CVJC

GRAPHIC SCIENCE

UNDERSTANDING

PHOTOSYNTHESIS

WITH MAX AXIOM SUPER SCIENTIST

by Liam O'Donnell

illustrated by Richard Dominguez

and Charles Barnett III

Consultant:
Dr. Ronald Browne
Associate Professor of Elementary Education
Minnesota State University, Mankato

Capstone
press

Mankato, Minnesota

Graphic Library is published by Capstone Press,
151 Good Counsel Drive, P.O. Box 669, Mankato, Minnesota 56002.
www.capstonepress.com

1 2 3 4 5 6 12 11 10 09 08 07

Library of Congress Cataloging-in-Publication Data
O'Donnell, Liam, 1970–
    Understanding photosynthesis with Max Axiom, super scientist / by Liam
O'Donnell; illustrated by Richard Dominguez and Charles Barnett III.
    p. cm.—(Graphic library. Graphic science.)
    Includes bibliographical references and index.
    ISBN-13: 978-0-7368-6841-9 (hardcover)
    ISBN-10: 0-7368-6841-0 (hardcover)
    ISBN-13: 978-0-7368-7893-7 (softcover pbk.)
    ISBN-10: 0-7368-7893-9 (softcover pbk.)
    1. Photosynthesis—Juvenile literature. I. Dominguez, Richard. II. Barnett, Charles
III. III. Title. IV. Series.
QK882.O34 2007
572'.46—dc22   2006029241

Summary: In graphic novel format, follows the adventures of Max Axiom as he explains
    the science behind photosynthesis.

Art Director and Designer
Bob Lentz

Cover Artist
Tod Smith

Colorist
Michael Kelleher

Editor
Donald Lemke

TABLE OF CONTENTS

While on his daily walk, Super Scientist Max Axiom discovers that all roads lead to plants.

Nothing's better than a long walk on a bright summer day.

Have you ever just stood and felt the sun on your face? It feels so warm.

Looks like I'm not the only one enjoying the sun!

But these sunflowers aren't just enjoying the sun. They're eating.

Before they can use the water, they need to break it down to the simplest atoms.

Plants need the water in these channels to start the process of photosynthesis.

Each molecule of water contains two hydrogen atoms and one oxygen atom.

HYDROGEN

HYDROGEN

OXYGEN

To see where plants take apart water molecules, let's jump inside a plant cell.

Inside every chloroplast are stacks of disks that contain a green substance called chlorophyll.

Chlorophyll captures energy from sunlight.

This energy causes the water molecules to split apart.

Oxygen atoms pair up and go one way.

Hydrogen atoms have another job. They mix with parts of the carbon dioxide, which the plant absorbed from the air.

Photosynthesis keeps animals healthy too.

Remember when the plant split the water molecule and used the hydrogen atoms to create food?

It didn't use the oxygen atoms that came from the water molecule.

The plant has no use for the extra oxygen, but we do.

Plants release the oxygen into the air through their tiny stomata or pores.

Whether you live in the countryside or in the city, plants and photosynthesis are important to keeping all living things healthy.

This natural process is fragile and can be easily damaged.

We live in a world of machines. Cars, trucks, and other machines make our lives easier.

But they use engines that release carbon dioxide into our air.

With so many engines in use, we are releasing more carbon dioxide than plants can absorb.

PHOTOSYNTHESIS

The main source of energy for every living thing is more than 93 million miles (150 million kilometers) away. Fortunately, energy from the sun travels extremely fast and takes only eight minutes to reach our planet.

Parts of the photosynthesis process can continue even without light from the sun. When the sun sets, plants still turn energy into sugars for food. This part of the process is known as the dark reaction phase.

Our planet has a wide variety of plant life. In fact, more than 260,000 species of plants grow on earth.

The Indian pipe plant has no chlorophyll. The flowering plant is completely white and has been called corpse plant or ghost flower. Lacking the ability to create food, the Indian pipe absorbs energy through its roots from fungi.

While some plants don't need sunlight, others don't need soil. Epiphyte plants dig their roots into trees or rocks for support. Moss, orchids, and other epiphytes often live high up on trees for better sunlight. Because of their location, they are sometimes called "air plants."

Planting a tree can have a major impact. One grown tree produces enough oxygen to support four people for a year.

Plants are the earth's only producers. Most other organisms are divided into three types of consumers:

Herbivores—animals that eat only plants
Carnivores—animals that eat other animals
Omnivores—animals that eat both plants and animals

 Plants can be carnivores. Some plants, including Venus flytraps and monkey cups, live where few nutrients are in the soil. They capture insects in their traps for food.

MORE ABOUT

SUPER SCIENTIST

Real name: Maxwell J. Axiom
Hometown: Seattle, Washington
Height: 6' 1"   Weight: 192 lbs
Eyes: Brown   Hair: None

Super capabilities: Super intelligence; able to shrink to the size of an atom; sunglasses give x-ray vision; lab coat allows for travel through time and space.

Origin: Since birth, Max Axiom seemed destined for greatness. His mother, a marine biologist, taught her son about the mysteries of the sea. His father, a nuclear physicist and volunteer park ranger, schooled Max on the wonders of earth and sky.

One day on a wilderness hike, a megacharged lightning bolt struck Max with blinding fury. When he awoke, Max discovered a newfound energy and set out to learn as much about science as possible. He traveled the globe earning degrees in every aspect of the field. Upon his return, he was ready to share his knowledge and new identity with the world. He had become Max Axiom, Super Scientist.

GLOSSARY

atmosphere (AT-muhss-feehr)—the mixture of gases that surrounds earth

atom (AT-uhm)—an element in its smallest form

carbon dioxide (KAHR-buhn dye-AHK-side)—a colorless, odorless gas that people and animals breathe out

chlorophyll (KLOER-uh-fil)—the green substance in plants that uses light to make food from carbon dioxide and water

hydrogen (HYE-druh-juhn)—a colorless gas that is lighter than air and burns easily

molecule (MOL-uh-kyool)—the atoms making up the smallest unit of a substance; H_2O is a molecule of water.

oxygen (OK-suh-juhn)—a colorless gas in the air that people and animals need to breathe

precipitation (pri-sip-i-TAY-shuhn)—water that falls from clouds to the earth's surface; precipitation can be rain, hail, sleet, or snow.

transpiration (transs-puh-RAY-shuhn)—the process by which plants give off moisture into the atmosphere

vascular (VASS-kew-luhr)—a system of channels for transporting fluids through plants

READ MORE

Biskup, Agnieszka. *Exploring Ecosystems with Max Axiom.* Graphic Science. Mankato, Minn.: Capstone Press, 2007.

Harman, Rebecca. *The Water Cycle.* Heinemann Infosearch. Chicago: Heinemann Library, 2005.

Juettner, Bonnie. *Photosynthesis.* The KidHaven Science Library. Detroit: KidHaven Press, 2005.

Kalman, Bobbie. *Food Chains and You.* Food Chains. New York: Crabtree, 2005.

Staub, Frank J. *Photosynthesis.* World of Wonder. Mankato, Minn.: Creative Education, 2003.

INTERNET SITES

FactHound offers a safe, fun way to find Internet sites related to this book. All of the sites on FactHound have been researched by our staff.

Here's how:
1. Visit *www.facthound.com*
2. Choose your grade level.
3. Type in this book ID **0736868410** for age-appropriate sites. You may also browse subjects by clicking on letters, or by clicking on pictures and words.
4. Click on the **Fetch It** button.

FactHound will fetch the best sites for you!

INDEX